WAVERLEY

The story of the World's last seagoing pad

Twelfth edition – April 2021
Published by Waverley Excursions Ltd., 36 Lancefield Quay, Glasgow, G3 8HA
waverleyexcursions.co.uk
ISBN 978-1-9168752-1-0

Photographs have been kindly provided by Eric Armstrong, Robin Boyd, Stuart Cameron, Hugh Dougherty, Graeme Dunlop, Tony Horn, David Howie, Douglas McGowan MBE, Murray Paterson, Graeme Phanco, Chris Phillips, Photononstop, Eddie Quinn, Iain Quinn, Keith Robertson, Bert Scott, Paul Semple, Ian Shannon, Margaret Skee, Roy Tait, Gordon Wilson, John Goss PSPS Collection, Paddle Steamer Preservation Society Collection, & Waverley Rebuild Collection.

Welcome Aboard!

Congratulations for wanting to know more about the *Waverley* – she is an exceptional ship!

Waverley has always collected marks of distinction. Since she was new there has been a plaque on board highlighting that our ship 'replaced' an earlier *Waverley* sunk by enemy action at Dunkirk. She has been the last sea-going paddle steamer in the world since 1970. She is the sole survivor of a vast fleet of passenger steamships that once provided coastal services and excursions all around the British coast. She is listed on the National Historic Ships Register of the UK.

Waverley is living history. The shipbuilding and engineering traditions of the past and the social history of Glasgow and the West of Scotland are all represented by the ship.

We know *Waverley* wins over the hearts and minds of everyone who encounters her. People like to see her around! The bright red of the funnels, her striking profile and the sight and sound of the paddles, can transform the dullest harbour and enhance even the loveliest scenery. People love to sail on her even more. She has open decks, period decoration and magnificent steam machinery open to view. She has everything needed for a wonderful day out, and she provides what is now rare access to the coasts and waters of the Firth of Clyde and wherever else she may be sailing.

Waverley is owned by a charity dedicated to keeping her sailing so that future generations can enjoy being on a real paddle steamer, but it's not easy to make the hands of time stand still. Charitable donations, passengers buying tickets and sales of memorabilia are all needed to make this possible.

We are proud that against all the odds *Waverley's* preservation career is now much longer than the time she spent as a 'commercial' ship. In 2019 there was a crisis with the season being missed and new boilers being needed. The response to our appeal to 'Save the *Waverley*' was magnificent and two new 'badges' were earned as *Waverley* was labelled both a 'National Treasure' and 'The People's Paddle Steamer' along the way. The COVID-19 pandemic followed on closely and brought its own challenges. But *Waverley* is still sailing!

If you bought your copy of this book at the ship's shop – enjoy your day on board! If it came in the post – make sure you book your own trip very soon. Either way, why not check out how you can become a Friend of Waverley?

I do hope you enjoy reading *Waverley's* story.

Derek Peters
Chairman
Waverley Steam Navigation Co Ltd
April 2021

Waverley goes to War

Above: 1899 Waverley *at War (May 1940)*

In time of war, the Clyde steamers have played a vital role in the defence of this country. An earlier *Waverley* saw service in both World Wars and is shown above in April 1940 off the south coast of England in the company of the Caledonian Steam Packet's *Duchess of Fife*. The *Fife* returned to the Clyde but Waverley paid the supreme sacrifice on 29th May 1940 when returning with troops from the Dunkirk beaches. (In passing, it is interesting to record that the remains of *Waverley* were found by a Belgian diver in the summer of 1985 and a few artefacts salvaged before leaving her in peace again.)

The London and North Eastern Railway (L.N.E.R.) lost two ships during the hostilities - *Waverley* and another paddle steamer, *Marmion*. Plans to replace both were drawn up and then shelved, with only one ship being built. This was the present *Waverley*.

The order went to A.&J. Inglis Ltd. in 1866 the yard had built the first two Clyde Steamers for the North British Railway (NB) and eighty years later work started on the first paddler for the L.N.E.R., successor to the NB, and the last for the Clyde.

In all, the Inglis Yard at Pointhouse, Glasgow, turned out eleven ships for the north bank services from Helensburgh and Craigendoran. The yard's final contribution to the Clyde steamer fleet came in 1953 when the motorships *Maid of Argyll* and *Maid of Skelmorlie* joined the CSP fleet. Inglis also constructed the last paddle steamer to be built for passenger traffic in the British Isles – Loch Lomond's *Maid of the Loch*.

Below: 1899 Waverley *during her peacetime days when she was ranked among the fastest of the Clyde Steamers (1919-1931 condition)*

The build

A. & J. Inglis undertook the conversion back to civilian service of the two L.N.E.R. paddlers that survivied active duty – the impressive *Jeanie Deans* dating from 1931, and the unique and perpetually-shaking *Talisman*, a diesel-electric paddler built by Inglis in 1935. The reconstruction produced ships considerably altered from their 1939 layout and appearance and the new paddler's plans closely followed the general scheme of the rehabilitated Jeanie. A misty 2nd October, 1946, saw the last paddle steamer to be built for the Clyde services named by Lady Matthews, wife of the L.N.E.R. Chairman.

The choice of the name *Waverley* perpetuated the memory of the North

British flier of 1899 and a suitable plaque was placed on the new ship. The north bank steamers were traditionally named after the novels or characters from the works of Sir Walter Scott.

The new *Waverley* was to be a shade smaller than the 1931 Jeanie. Her length, for example, at 240' was 11' less and her passenger certificate allowed 1,350 as against 1,480. First and second class accommodation was provided including a dining saloon, lounge, tearoom and shop on the main deck with a bar and tearoom on the lower deck. Two large deck shelters were constructed on the promenade

Bottom left: Hull no. 1330 during construction
Below: Construction with the paddlebox in view & the large opening can be seen to allow the engine and boiler to be fitted later
Bottom: Waverley's keel looking forward

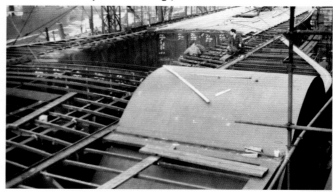

deck with the bridge, wheelhouse, master's room and two lifeboats placed over the forward shelter. Passengers shared the deck above the after shelter with two lifeboats and the mainmast.

Once the fitting out of *Waverley* was well advanced, the new steamer was towed from Pointhouse to Greenock's Victoria Harbour where Rankin & Blackmore fitted the double-ended boiler and the magnificent triple-expansion steam engine. She was fitted with 18-ft diameter rimless paddle wheels each with eight flat wooden feathering floats. For her first ten years, *Waverley* was coal-fired but in 1957 her boiler was converted to burn heavy fuel oil.

Top right: Waverley's *Launch 2nd October 1946*

Bottom right: The new Waverley *afloat after launching*

Left: At Pointhouse Yard after her launch. Talisman *can be seen in the background.*

Bottom left: Waverley's *engine are completed and ready to be dismantled and taken to the ship for reassembly*

Above: The completed Dining Saloon which was used as a workshop for constructing the duckboards for the paddlebox landing platforms and Bridge

The L.N.E.R. eschewed the CSP practice of the 1930s of disguising the paddleboxes of their steamers and *Waverley* carries a fan-vented paddlebox of traditional appearance with scroll work and figurehead of Scott's hero, Edward Waverley.

In 1947, *Waverley* was one of a multitude of steamers fitted with triple expansion engines. Now, she is alone in her class. The experience of gazing on the three massive pistons and cranks as they silently and effortlessly propel the vessel is reserved today only for those on board *Waverley*.

Bottom left: Waverley at Victoria Harbour ready for the boilers and engine to be installed
Bottom right: Waverley during sea trials in June 1947 when a top speed of 18.5 knots was attained with the engine running at 56 rpm. In service 15 knots is usually adequate but a reserve is there if the need arises.

Waverley in her element

Top right: Waverley's *first day in service, 16th June 1947*
Above: Waverley *in Rothesay Bay in her first season - 17th June 1947*
Left: A rare colour photograph of Waverley *in the summer of 1947*

The new paddle steamer was to take her share of the ferry work from Craigendoran to the Clyde Coast resorts but *Waverley's* maiden voyage on Monday 16th June, 1947 was on the route for which she was primarily intended – the cruise up Loch Goil and Loch Long to the villages of Lochgoilhead and Arrochar. The sailing was part of the popular Three Lochs Tour which allowed the traveller to enjoy a circular tour including a sail on one of

7

the Loch Lomond paddlers from Balloch at the south end to Tarbet. From Tarbet the excursionist crossed, on foot or by coach, the narrow strip of land separating the freshwater Loch Lomond from the sealoch Loch Long. At Arrochar, *Waverley* was joined to complete another part of the circle via Loch Long and Loch Goil. Lochgoilhead Pier was the link in two circular tours available in certain years to passengers on *Waverley*. A coach left Lochgoilhead for Inveraray going via Rest-and-be-Thankful. One of the swift turbine steamers, usually *Duchess of Montrose*, was boarded at Inveraray for the return leg of the journey. Another possibility was to travel by coach from Dunoon via Loch Eck and Hell's Glen to Lochgoilhead where *Waverley* would be waiting.

Waverley sailed to Arrochar six times a week in 1947 but in the last year Arrochar Pier was in use, 1972, the frequency had dropped to once weekly. In July 1965 Lochgoilhead Pier was closed, having been declared unsafe, and soon thereafter was dismantled.

Captain John E Cameron D.S.C and Chief Engineer William Summers joined *Waverley* in 1947. Captain Cameron left Waverley in 1948 and Captain Donald Crawford took command for a time. Bill Summers remained with *Waverley* until his retirement came in 1969. When Waverley Steam Navigation Co. Ltd. took over the paddler in 1974, it was clear that *Waverley* had become more than a job to Bill who welcomed the chance to get close again to his engines and he made his years of experience available to the new owners. His contribution was significant during those difficult years. Bill Summers passed away in 1977 and John Cameron eleven years later, but their enthusiasm for the ship's preservation is widely acknowledged.

Change - for the better?

Below: Spring of 1948 at Bowling Harbour and Waverley's L.N.E.R. funnel colours disappear

Waverley was allowed only one season to sail in the attractive L.N.E.R. colours. Her hull and paddleboxes were black while the former carried two gold lines immediately beneath the cream topsides. The deck shelters were grained brown. Above towered red funnels with black tops and white bands.

At the end of 1947 the various privately-owned railway companies were grouped into a nationalised British Transport Commission (BTC) and the need for uniformity rode roughshod over aesthetic considerations. The bright funnel colours of the L.N.E.R. were painted over with the drab buff and black of the BTC. The Clyde would wait a quarter of a century before once again seeing the red, white and black.

In November 1951 the Craigendoran paddlers – *Jeanie Deans, Talisman* and *Waverley* – were transferred to the Commission's Scottish shipping subsidiary, The Caledonian Steam Packet Co. Ltd. This allowed the eventual replacement of the buff by more-pleasing Caley bright yellow.

The 1951 change in ownership affected each of the ships differently. The *Jeanie* saw minimal change and was seldom asked to carry out tasks alien to a "north bank" steamer. *Talisman,* on the other hand, was re-engined within three years and became the regular steamer in summer on the Caledonian Wemyss Bay-Largs-Millport-Kilchattan Bay service.

The integration of *Waverley* into the CSP fleet was gradual and she saw increasing service on the ferry routes from Gourock and Wemyss Bay. Her cruising programme in summer was widened at the expense of Arrochar trips. In 1953, *Waverley* began a Monday sailing from Craigendoran through

the Kyles of Bute to Brodick, Lamlash and Whiting Bay. This excursion remained with her until 1971. Lamlash Pier was closed at the end of 1954 and Whiting Bay went likewise in 1961 and *Waverley* latterly called at Brodick and then sailed towards Pladda at the south end of Arran.

In 1955 *Waverley* revived an excursion with Caledonian origins when she sailed "Round the Lochs" on Wednesdays. Three days later

Right: Waverley *approaching Dunoon Pier in the late 1960's. The British Rail colour scheme is visible with the hull painted blue.*

our steamer fell heir to a day-trip introduced in 1957 by the turbine *Marchioness of Graham*. This was the "Up-River" sailing from Largs, Rothesay and Dunoon to Glasgow. The *Graham* had been sold out of fleet and so Friday visits to Glasgow (Bridge Wharf) became a regular feature of *Waverley's* summer programme.

Waverley now even deputised occasionally on the turbine steamer cruises from Gourock and Glasgow. From 1958 to 1962 she took the Gourock cruises of *Duchess of Hamilton* for the closing weeks of the season. Alan Brown in his book "Craigendoran Steamers" recalls:" *Waverley* probably reached her peak in the late fifties when, under the command of Captain Colin MacKay and with Bill Summers at the throttle, she achieved an enviable reputation for punctuality and general smartness. Friday, 26th September, 1958 was an outstanding day in *Waverley's* career, for on that day she was rostered for the the first time to take the Gourock-Ayr sailing, with its associated cruise round Holy Isle. She had deputised for *Duchess of Hamilton* the whole of that week and it was obvious that the Mackay/Summers team was determined to put up a good show on the exacting long cruises.

"Throughout the week *Waverley* had maintained excellent timings, and great interest centred on the Ayr run, for it was on this that she faced her stiffest task. It was therefore with considerable anticipation and excitement that I made my way down to Gourock Pier that calm, crisp, sunny autumn morning; nor was I disappointed, for *Waverley* gave me the most enjoyable and thrilling sail I have had on the Clyde in post-war days. The whole day was tightly scheduled, but nevertheless she arrived at Ayr in ample time to commence her afternoon cruise round Holy Isle at 1.45pm. Leaving Ayr one minute late on the return run to Gourock she pounded homewards, her triple cranks spinning round at an effortless 50 rpm and her wooden floats endlessly repeating their intoxicating "eight beats to the bar" rhythm.

"Slicing through the dark, glassy water, she left a broad carpet of foam trailing astern, and as she curved round into Gourock there was a general air of triumph on board. Alongside the pier *Duchess of Hamilton* lay at peace, and on the after deck a number of her crew were seated, perhaps speculating on the hour of *Waverley's* return. The look of utter astonishment and blank disbelief on their faces as *Waverley* berthed, three minutes ahead of schedule, still remains as a vivid memory of September 26th, 1958."

If Alan Brown is correct and *Waverley* was at her peak in the late fifties, she quickly fell into a trough in the early sixties. The standard day-to-day maintenance dropped and the ship presented a very down-at-heel appearance. Colin MacKay had retired early in 1960 and a less steady hand was at the helm. After some years of neglect *Waverley*'s fortunes took a turn for the better as more energetic hands took control.

Top: Waverley *approaching Innellan 1963-1964*
Below left: Waverley *arriving at Dunoon Pier 1959*
Below right: Waverley *departing Gourock with White Paddle Boxes 1961*

Starting in the 1961 summer, *Waverley* and her older sister *Jeanie Deans* began alternating on the Craigendoran excursions. This meant *Waverley* spent every other week on the afternoon Round Bute cruise. *Jeanie Deans* had been in decline for many years but towards the end of the Clyde career a change in personnel and duties put some pep back into the old girl and there was some hotly-contested sprints as both paddlers headed home in the evening.

Jeanie Deans was withdrawn at the end of September 1964 and the next season found the paddle steamer *Caledonia* at Craigendoran with *Waverley*. The two paddlers alternated on the Wednesday Round the Lochs but otherwise tended to perform the same duties each week with *Waverley* sailing Round Bute on Monday, to Arrochar on Tuesday and Thursday, and up-river to Glasgow on Friday. On Saturday and Sunday both steamers operated from Craigendoran.

Waverley's former stablemate, *Talisman,* shook her last late in 1966. The next summer, *Waverley's* Sunday duties were recast to include *Talisman's* popular afternoon sailing from Millport and Largs to Rothesay and Tighnabruaich. This arrangement held for the next two seasons.

Below left: The two paddlers Waverley *and* Caledonia *at Craigendoran Pier*
Below right: Aboard Waverley *in the late 1960s*

Colour Schemes

Change in ownership forced *Waverley* to abandon the L.N.E.R. livery in early 1948. The British Transport Commission's funnel colours of dull buff and black tops were adopted.
The Caledonian Steam Packet's imprint was seen in 1953 when the deck saloons were painted white and the ventilators, previously grained, were now silver with blue interiors.

Top right: Dunoon, 1958 with the ventilators painted silver with blue interiors

Above: Rothesay Bay in 1959
Bottom right: 1962 after both Funnels had been replaced

The paddleboxes of *Waverley* became white in late May 1959. In common with the other CSP cruise vessels, radar was fitted before the 1960 summer. Metal corrosion caused the replacement of *Waverley*'s funnels in two stages: the forward funnel in 1961 and aft funnel in 1962. The new ones, which were welded rather than riveted, were much heavier than their predecessors, and the extra weight caused a slight sag in the deck resulting in the funnels being marginally out of alignment.

British Rail introduced a new colour scheme for their fleets in 1965 and this was adopted in part by the railway-owned Clyde Steamers. The hulls were painted blue while deck railings and ventilators became grey. Instead of the BR red funnel, rather small red Caledonian lions rampant were fitted to the yellow funnels.

In January 1969, the CSP became a subsidiary of the Scottish Transport Group and after that summer the hulls reverted to black.

By 1972, *Waverley* was the sole surviving Clyde paddler and to

Top right: Waverley *at Lochranza in 1971 with a half mast. She was blown against the Pier at Arrochar and the mast snapped. She sailed the rest of the 1971 season like this.*

Middle right: Waverley *on charter to the Paddle Steamer Preservation Society in 1972 at Inveraray*

Bottom right: Waverley *departing Dunoon in 1973 in Caledonian MacBrayne Funnel Colours*

Left: "Paddle Down the Clyde the Waverley *Way" leaflet for the 1972 season*

accentuate her uniqueness, the paddle boxes were painted black. A new flag and funnel colouring in 1973 reflected the union of the Caledonian S.P. Co. with much of David MacBrayne Ltd. into Caledonian MacBrayne Ltd. Funnels were red with black tops (MacBrayne) and bore yellow discs with red lions (Caledonian).

The end of an era?

Waverley's regular routine in the summer of 1973 included the Round Bute sail on Sundays, Mondays, and Thursdays – from Gourock though, not Craigendoran which was closed after the 1972 summer season. On Tuesdays and Wednesdays she gave the Round the Lochs day cruise while on Fridays Tarbert was the destination. Saturdays were spent on ferry work in the morning with an afternoon cruise to Tighnabruaich. *Waverley* gave a number of Showboat Evening cruises from Largs and Rothesay to the Kyles of Bute. On Mondays from 28th May to 9th July further variety was introduced when *Waverley* was allocated the morning commuter run from Brodick to Ardrossan since no other vessel was available.

As the 1973 season drew to a close, clearly *Waverley's* future was in question and two enthusiasts' groups arranged special sailings. The Clyde River Steamer Club had the ship on Saturday 15th September and called at Brodick and Campbeltown. Two weeks later, the Paddle Steamer Preservation Society took on a Five Lochs Cruise visiting the Holy Loch plus Lochs Riddon, Striven, Long and Goil. *Waverley's* last day in service for Caledonian MacBrayne, Sunday 30th September, was spent being filmed in the morning and later sailing round Bute. On 1st October, she entered James Watt Dock, Greenock, for lay-up.

Waverley's track record in 1973 had not been good. Nine days' sailings had been cancelled because of mechanical trouble and her schedule had been interrupted on many other occasions. The motor ship *Maid of Argyll* had been available to cover for both *Waverley* and *Queen Mary II* but the *Argyll* was on the Sale List and would leave for the Mediterranean in April 1974.

The results of the 1973 cruising programme were described in the Scottish Transport Group's Annual report as "particularly disappointing" (even though *Waverley* carried more passengers in 1973 than in any of the preceding ten years). The prospect of operating two ageing, unreliable and expensive cruise ships on the Clyde was too much for the STG and the 1974 Clyde excursion programme was to be curtailed to a single ship – *Queen Mary II*. The STG report continues, "As a result of this decision, the *PS Waverley* had been taken out of service and, as the last sea-going paddler, has been offered for preservation".

Below: Waverley *in 1973 off Largs*

Sold for £1

Perhaps today a pound can't buy much but in August 1974 it bought a 693-ton paddle steamer!

The Scottish Transport Group recognised that the withdrawal of *Waverley* marked the end of an era stretching from 1812 when Henry Bell's little paddler *Comet* sailed from Glasgow. The Paddle Steamer Preservation Society (PSPS) had been actively interested in *Waverley* for a number of years. The two organisations came together in November 1973 and, through Caledonian MacBrayne, the STG offered the vessel to the PSPS. At that time there was no thought of returning the steamer to service, rather she was to become a static restaurant/museum operation.

But a static, silent steamer is a poor substitute for a vibrant, moving, alive paddler.

By the end of 1973, Terry Sylvester and Douglas McGowan, two active and optimistic members of the PSPS, were investigating ways of returning *Waverley* to service and within a few months the local authorities were approached with a novel idea. The last seagoing paddle steamer could be a tourist attraction for the south west region of Scotland. The City of Glasgow, Strathclyde Region and others were invited to join in the experiment of running a paddle steamer.

On 8th August 1974, *Waverley* was officially handed over by Calmac to Waverley Steam Navigation Company Ltd., a company formed by the PSPS. The price tag was one pound and was satisfied by a donation from Sir Patrick Thomas, chairman of the STG.

Left: Douglas McGowan (WSN), John Whittle (CalMac), Sir Patrick Thomas (STG) & Terry Sylvester (WSN) with the £1 note that bought Waverley *on 8th August 1974*

That was the easy part. *Waverley* lay idle in the James Watt Dock while her fate was debated in the council chambers around the country. But the enthusiasts were not idle. Recognising the "put up or shut up" challenge from the STG, PSPS members and friends formed working parties and set about cleaning up the ship and ticking off items on a long maintenance list.

The marketing of *Waverley* as a Scottish asset began right away and the funnels were returned to their pristine red, white and black. This allowed a public appeal to be launched for funds to add to an anonymous gift of £10,000 and then £11,000 from Glasgow Corporation.

If *Waverley* was to sail in the summer of 1975 she had to be drydocked for survey and major repairs. No word had come from the newly-formed Strathclyde Region about the funds essential for *Waverley's* future. Waverley S.N.Co. took a gamble (not to be the last!) and booked their steamer into Scotts' Garvel Drydock on 17th February 1975 for a four-week stay.

During the drydocking the welcome announcement came of a £30,000 grant from Strathclyde Region. *Waverley* would sail again. Harrisons (Clyde) were appointed as the ship's technical managers and this added credibility to the venture at a time when sceptics were not hard to find.

By April 1975, officers and crew were being engaged. The public appeal had raised over £40,000 and the Scottish Tourist Board added £30,000.

The fires were lit on 10th May 1975 and five days later *Waverley* moved out of dock for trials.

Right: Invitation to Waverley's *inaugural voyage in Preservation 1975*
Below left: Waverley *in James Watt dock early in W.S.N Co. Ltd. ownership*
Below right: City of Glasgow Police Pipe Band perform on her invited guests sailing

The Directors of
Waverley Steam Navigation Co. Ltd.
have pleasure in inviting

aboard their paddle steamer,

"WAVERLEY"

on Thursday, 22nd May, 1975
on the occasion of the steamer's special inaugural voyage.

R.S.V.P. by 15 May to :
DOUGLAS McGOWAN,
49 Stanmore Road,
Glasgow, G42 9AJ.   Steamer departs Anderston Quay 2 p.m. arriving back 7 p.m.

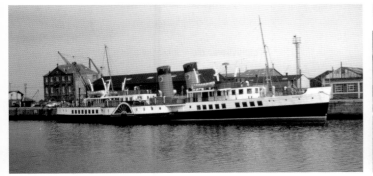

After an extremely busy seven days, the City of Glasgow Police Pipe Band gave *Waverley* a magnificent send off for her first passenger sailing on Thursday 22nd May 1975. All who had helped in some way return *Waverley* to service were on board for the sail from Glasgow to Dunoon. Her first public cruise, on the 24th, was from Glasgow to Tarbert and Ardrishaig.

Five weeks of charter and public sailings followed before *Waverley* took up her regular summer timetable. With unusual prescience, the STG had included a "non-competitive" clause in the Sale Agreement. This forced *Waverley* into cruising territory abandoned years before by the nationalised body as uneconomic. In July and August 1975, *Waverley* was based for four days each week at the busy commercial port of Ayr and at Glasgow three days. Day Excursions were offered and in addition to calls at the usual piers, the timetable included Troon, Greenock and Kilcreggan.

Above: Waverley's *first public sailing in Preservation departing Ardrishaig 24th May 1975*
Left: Waverley *departing Stranraer 27th June 1976*

(It was 1979 before dredging opened up Helensburgh Pier for regular calls by *Waverley*). The return of *Waverley* in 1975 meant that Clyde cruising had become a possibility again for a large section of the population and visitors in south-west Scotland.

The ingenuity of the WSN timetable, the effectiveness of the publicity and the excellent summer weather combined to produce several days when passengers had to be turned away. Even though boiler trouble occasionally disrupted sailings, Waverley carried over 121,000 excursionists before the season ended on Monday 8th September and *Waverley* laid up at Glasgow for the winter.

Above: Waverley & Queen Mary *at Anderston Quay, Glasgow 1976*

By the end of the 1975 summer it was recognised that *Waverley* could be more than a nine-day wonder. Many had assumed the venture would fold sometime in June with money, energy, patience and credit exhausted, but the ship and those involved persevered and the possibility was seen for *Waverley* having a long term future in Clyde cruising.

But financial hurdles remained. Strathclyde Regional Council decided against any financial support for *Waverley* in 1976 despite a strong recommendation from consultants hired by them to investigate Clyde cruising as part of the Region's tourist industry. The Regional Council put its money behind Caledonian MacBrayne – first *Queen Mary* and later *Glen Sannox*. The turbine

Queen Mary lasted two more seasons before being withdrawn.

As we know, *Waverley* survived, thanks to help from various District Councils – Glasgow being foremost among them – the Scottish Tourist Board and many, many individuals.

Part of the deal struck between CalMac and Strathclyde Region in the Spring of 1976 required the return of *Queen Mary* to Glasgow on three days a week, putting the two ships in direct competition. A compromise was reached but on Sunday mornings that summer both the turbine and the paddler sailed from Glasgow – the first time since 1951 that two steamers had sailed regularly from Glasgow. *Waverley's* 1976 season was very successful with the ship being continuously in steam from 10th May to 22nd September and passenger carryings up 50 per cent – even with the Glasgow trade being shared with *Queen Mary*.

The Region's administrator favoured *Queen Mary* and *Glen Sannox* but the aficionado and the general public voted with their feet for *Waverley!* CalMac again abandoned Glasgow at the end of the 1979 season. *Waverley* sailed from Glasgow one day the following year with a broom (for clean sweeping!) at her masthead. The car ferry/cruise ship *Glen Sannox's* involvement in cruising slowly dwindled. In late 1980 CalMac announced the abandonment of all Clyde cruising, but later seasons found ferries such as *Glen Sannox, Jupiter* and *Keppel* on trips on the upper firth.

A bleak day

But it all nearly came to an end on Friday 15th July 1977.

Waverley was on her usual Friday sailing from Glasgow to Kilcreggan and Dunoon with a cruise to Loch Long and Loch Goil. Delays on the river in the morning, a tight schedule made even more so by adverse tides, an attempt to save precious minutes by swinging inside the Gantocks when approaching Dunoon from the north (it had worked easily on other occasions), the beginning of the ebb tide, a sluggish helm response, a list to port caused by people waiting to disembark; all combined to cause *Waverley* to bear down on one of the marker buoys off the Gantocks. The Captain took evasive action and rang down an emergency "Full Astern". The buoy was avoided but as the ship moved astern she caught on a pinnacle of Gantocks rock.

Waverley took water aft and the ebbing tide left her impaled. Passengers were quickly transferred to the ferry *Sound of Shuna* and landed at Dunoon Pier.

At midnight, *Waverley* floated off and was berthed at Dunoon Quay where the damage was inspected.

Major repairs in drydock were required and she was not back in service until Thursday 1st September, although the motor vessel *Queen of Scots* was chartered to cover as much of *Waverley's* schedule as possible. The loss of revenue from the best part of the season nearly proved fatal but, once again, *Waverley* survived to sail another day.

Widening horizons

The short operating season has always been a problem for the Clyde excursion steamers. In 1976, *Waverley* was in service for about eighteen weeks and in that time had to earn enough to keep her for a whole year. An exciting opportunity to extend the 1977 season came to WSN late in 1976. Llandudno Pier was to celebrate its centenary in May 1977 and Aberconwy Council offered to sponsor a visit by *Waverley* to the North Wales resort. The trip was declared feasible and plans were taking shape when Aberconwy Council withdrew as sponsors. Encouraged by initial responses, however, WSN decided to go ahead with the trip taking on the full financial responsibility. So, on Thursday 28th April 1977 *Waverley*, having revived the sailing from Campbeltown and Arran for the Ayr Agricultural Show earlier in the day, left Campbeltown just before midnight and turned south after clearing Davaar. *Waverley* reached Princes Landing Stage, Liverpool at 4.30pm on the Friday. Llandudno Pier celebrations were launched when *Waverley* called at 2pm on 1st May with a full load from Liverpool. A cruise was then given to Amlwch.

With the experience gained in the Mersey trip, WSN planned increasingly ambitious programmes. In the spring of 1978, *Waverley* sailed round Land's End for a four week stint of cruising on the South Coast, Isle of Wight, Thames and Medway. An even longer spell down south was made in April and May of 1979 and included five days on the Bristol Channel. The effect on the steamer's economics was quite dramatic. In 1979, *Waverley* carried 230,000 passengers, nearly double the 1975 figure. Of these, 66,000 had sailed on her while outside Scottish waters. Fleetwood was the first port of call on *Waverley's* 1980 trip south, an operation that included Liverpool, the South Coast, Thames and Medway, and the Bristol Channel. *Waverley* sailed from Deal on 12th May first to Cap Gris Nez and then followed one of the convoy routes used by the assorted flotilla that worked the miracle of the evacuation. Captain Cameron cast a wreath on the sea as memories went back to the day an earlier *Waverley* and much of her human cargo were finally defeated by repeated air attacks.

Top: Waverley *approaching Llandudno Pier , 1st May 1977 - the Pier Centenary Day*
Left: Captain John Cameron with the wreath to commemorate the Dunkirk evacuation
Bottom right: Waverley *at Princes Landing Stage, Liverpool, 30th April 1977*

Waverley's triple expansion steam engine

Sailing through London Tower Bridge

New lungs for an old lady

Above: Prince Ivanhoe *and* Waverley *at Stobcross Quay.* Waverley's *funnels can be seen on the quayside.*

In 1946 when the LNER and the A. & J. Inglis discussed the new paddle steamer, the question arose as to whether she would burn coal or oil. Economics dictated coal, and it was 1957 before *Waverley's* boiler was converted to oil burning.

Waverley had been plagued with boiler trouble during the latter part of her CalMac career, and this was seen as the ship's one weakness when she passed into WSN ownership. *Waverley's* engineers fought their way to the end of the 1975 season and in the spring of 1976 a complete retubing of the 29-year-old boiler was done. This produced a great improvement, but the measure was only a stop-gap. A new boiler was what was required, but the funds were just not available.

No one needs to be told of the astronomical increase in fuel costs in the 1970s. If *Waverley* was to have a future, reboilering was essential. In 1980 it was agreed to proceed with a new boiler. The problem was, of course, the lack of ready cash to meet the expected cost of £180,000 plus – even with much of the work being done by the ship's staff.

Chief Engineer Ken Blacklock and his team set to in late 1980 and began the preliminary work. Early in March 1981 all was ready. After the funnels were removed by a mobile crane at Stobcross Quay, she was towed the short distance up river to the Finnieston Crane where the old boiler came out on 10th March and the new one, constructed by Babcock Power Ltd. of Renfrew, was installed six days later. The advantages were immediate: improved speed, 1981's fuel costs were down 17% from 1980, steam was raised in minutes rather than hours, and bunkers were taken less frequently. The new boiler exhausts only through the forward funnel, while the after one houses fan intakes and generator exhausts.

Above: Waverley with her funnels awaiting her new boiler at Stobcross Quay
Below: New boiler is lowered into position

Above: New Babcock boiler arrives with the 1947 boiler behind
Below: Boiler in position

Round Britain Cruise

Complete with new boiler, her 1981 season would make history when she became the first coastal steamer to sail round Britain offering excursions at various ports on her way round, which would have proven too much of a challenge for her original boiler.

In April 1981, *Waverley,* made what was at that time her longest continuous voyage – Glasgow to Poole in Dorset – in 35 hours. The new boiler removed any need for expensive bunkering stops. It was two months before *Waverley* churned the waters of the Clyde again. The spring sailings were destined to encounter severe weather – wind, rain and even snow, but the people turned out regardless. An evening cruise on Friday 24th April from Poole and Bournemouth opened the "Steaming round Britain" programme. A week later, *Waverley* was on the Medway for a couple of days before moving to London. Saturday 2nd May was a marathon. Waverley sailed from London's Tower Pier at 0700 to Cap Gris Nez, calling at Greenwich, Tilbury, Southend and Ramsgate. She returned to the capital at 0100 next morning – 18 hours steaming, with a full complement on the cross-Channel leg. Monday 4th was the May Day Holiday and *Waverley* gave a day trip from London to Gillingham on the Medway.

The following day saw *Waverley's* final Thames cruise for 1981 and she then headed up the east coast. In the following weeks excursions were given from Hull, Goole, New Holland, Newcastle, North and South Shields with calls at Scarborough and Middlesborough. The final sailing in this part of the country was on Monday 25th May, the Spring Bank Holiday, when *Waverley* sailed from Newcastle, South and North Shields

round the Farne Islands. By the next evening, *Waverley* had sailed into the Firth of Forth and cruised from Granton (acting as Edinburgh's port) under the Bridges. *Waverley* had some busy days on the Forth especially on the sailings round the Bass Rock (30th May) and round the Isle of May and St. Andrews Bay (31st May).

Waverley left the Firth of Forth and set course for Duncansby Head, then through the infamous Pentland Firth and round Cape Wrath. Heading down the west coast a call was made at Kyle of Lochalsh and early on the morning of Thursday 4th June Oban Bay heard a paddle beat for the first time in nearly 40 years. The same day passengers joined the paddler for

Top: Waverley's *first visit to Crinan in 1985*
Left: Sailing under the Forth Bridges

the single trip to Ayr calling at Islay's Port Ellen. Her arrival at Ayr at 2200 completed her circuit of Great Britain.

Three days later she was off to the Bristol Channel, sailing down the east coast of Ireland to shelter from the strong westerly wind. Late on 22nd June *Waverley* sailed from Penarth on her way back to Scotland.

The cruising schedule drawn up for *Waverley* in 1981 emphasises the change in fortune that has befallen the ship. What greater contrast can there be between *Waverley* in 1947 – a steamer that for her first years in service did not possess a passenger certificate allowing her beyond the Cumbrae Heads – and *Waverley* in 1981 – a steamer circumnavigating Britain? We also reflect that in 1973 she had been cast aside as having no further role to play in this country's tourist industry.

She undertook two more "Round Britain" marathons, clockwise in 1982 and anti-clockwise in 1983.

Left: Waverley *at Girvan Harbour 1982*
Bottom left: Waverley *in Newcastle*
Top right: Waverley *at Tenby, 1991*
Bottom right: Waverley *sailing through the Narrows, 1982*

From Portland Bill to the Pool of London

Above: Waverley *waits for London Tower Bridge to open, 1984*
Below: Waverley *at Bournemouth Pier, 1991*

Paddle steamer sailings on the South Coast continued well into the 1960s. After a gap of a decade or so, *Waverley* revived this tradition of visiting the South Coast waters, and has maintained a presence in the area ever since. One of the most memorable days *Waverley* has spent on the South Coast was 17th September 1982 when the paddler was a floating grandstand for over 1000 people at the emotional return to Portsmouth of HMS Invincible after the Falklands Campaign. The commemoration in 1990 of the 50th Anniversary of the Dunkirk evacuation involved *Waverley* to an even greater extent than that of ten years previously. On Thursday 24th May she accompanied the "little ships" from Dover across the Channel and took part in a wreath-laying ceremony close to the French Coast.

Three days later she took her passengers, again from Dover, to the Beaches Remembrance Service off Dunkirk and the weekend was rounded off on the Monday by her sailing from Ramsgate to meet the "little ships" returning.

Pre-war, Ramsgate was the destination of several London-based excursion vessels such as Royal Sovereign and Royal Eagle, and *Waverley* follows in their wake.

Leaving from the Pool of London she first passes under the raised arms of the iconic Tower Bridge. This is in vivid contrast to the style of the Thames Flood Barrier which was built in the 1980s. A regular calling point for *Waverley* is the mile-and-a-quarter long Southend Pier – the longest pleasure pier in the world.

To the Scottish Isles & across the Irish Sea

Waverley's first passenger sailings in Highland waters were a minor part of the "Steaming Round Britain" programme in 1981. Most years, around the May Day Holiday weekend, she offers a short season of cruises based at Oban and visiting such places as Fort William and Iona, with the first visit in fifty years by a paddler to the Sacred Isle being given on a Saturday 24th April 1982. The 1988 Western Isles season was extended to include Mallaig, Kyle of Lochalsh and Portree, but this paled into insignificance when compared to the following year's developments. The last time a paddler had been seen in the Outer Hebrides was in October 1943 when Pioneer had called at Tarbert (Harris) on livestock sailings. Paddle steamer excursion sailings in this area were almost unheard of, so Waverley's 1989 visit to Lochmaddy, Tarbert and Stornoway was indeed a historic event.

Top: Waverley *approaching Armadale, Skye 1991*
Below: Passengers disembark at Douglas, Isle of Man 1991

In April of 1985, *Waverley* paid her first visit to a foreign country when several days were spent sailing from ports in Eire. During this time, the Irish tricolor was flown as a courtesy flag. Pursers, catering and souvenir shop staff faced the unprecedented hazards of pricing in Irish punts! She returned the following year sailing from, among other places, Dublin, Cork and Youghal. Northern Ireland had to wait a further five years to welcome the last sea-going paddle steamer, a weekend of sailings being given from Belfast.

Waverley has taken day trippers to the Isle of Man from Scotland (Garlieston), Ulster (Donaghadee) and England (Whitehaven) and has also performed coastal cruises and sailings right round the island. Passengers on the first Garlieston sailing in 1985 received an unexpected bonus when their (Friday) "day trip" became a weekend. The outward journey was lively but continued bad weather precluded her return until 0600 on the Monday morning. In more recent years the steamer has cruised from Ayr and Campbeltown across the North Channel to Red Bay on the Antrim Coast.

Westward Ho!

The Bristol Channel had long been a paddle steamer preserve. A summer charter on the Bristol Channel in 1887 had taken an earlier *Waverley* away from her Clyde duties. Her owners, Peter and Alec Campbell decided to transfer their activities to the area and the name of P.&A. Campbell became synonymous with the Channel steamers. The last paddler of the line, *Bristol Queen*, was withdrawn in August 1967 and thereafter motorships, latterly *Balmoral*, kept the Campbell flag flying until October 1980.

The 1947 *Waverley* brought the sound of paddles back to the Channel in May 1979 when the paddler had five successful days of cruising. Early spring before beginning the main Clyde programme, *Waverley* gave a short season of excursions on the Channel. Her usual schedule includes most of the traditional calling points, with Ilfracombe, while the island of Lundy, 12 miles from Devon coast, receives annual visits.

The historic port of Bristol is approached by navigating the narrow twisting River Avon, with its notorious Horseshoe Bend and spectacular Gorge. *Waverley's* first visit to the city was in October 1986. Waverley's visit to the Padstow in 1988 was the first by a paddle steamer for 21 years. On Saturday 27th May 1989 the paddler gave three special cruises from Clevedon to mark the re-opening of its Victorian pier.

Balmoral was rescued by W.S.N. Co. Ltd. and brought to Glasgow for a major refit. In April 1986 Balmoral resumed her sailings on the Bristol Channel where she continued to provide the main summer programme of cruises. After 25 years of ownership and due to poor weather performance and lost revenue, W.S.N Co. Ltd took the difficult decision in 2012 to withdraw Balmoral from service. Today, Balmoral is owned by the charity MV Balmoral Fund Limited who are working towards restoring Balmoral to full pleasure steaming operation.

Top: Balmoral *and* Waverley *on the Bristol Channel*
Below: Waverley *landing at Lundy Island 1985*
Bottom: Waverley *going astern Ilfracombe*

Kingswear Castle

It was as long ago as 1967 that the Paddle Steamer Preservation Society purchased the small paddle steamer *Kingswear Castle*. She dates from 1924 and so is *Waverley's* senior by 23 years. The 110' steamer is propelled by a compound diagonal engine built in 1904 and transferred to *Kingswear Castle* from an earlier paddler of the same name. This makes the engine one of the oldest marine engines to survive in Britain.

In 1924, the coal-fired *Kingswear Castle* joined a fleet of three small paddlers and two screw motorships on the picturesque River Dart. During the Second World War she was requisitioned and served as a tender at Dartmouth for both Royal and U.S. Navies. By 1964 *Kingswear Castle* was the last surviving Dart paddler.

She was laid up at the end of the 1965 season and acquired by the PSPS in 1967 for restoration. Progress was slow but the success of *Waverley* gave the *Kingswear Castle* project a needed credibility and impetus. After years of work by volunteers, the paddler sailed under her own power again in November 1983. She was now far from the River Dart and it was the River Medway that frothed under her paddle beat.

During the 1984 summer a limited programme of sailings was offered from Strood on the Medway. It was 1985 before a full passenger certificate was obtained for *Kingswear Castle*, and a summer of sailings from the Medway piers and Southend was achieved.

In December 2012 *Kingswear Castle* returned to her home waters on the River Dart after an absence of 45 years. Still coal-fired, Kingswear Castle sails from Dartmouth and Totnes. Her main sailings are 90 minute Dartmouth Harbour cruises but on selected days she steams up the beautiful River Dart to Totnes and back on long term charter to the Dartmouth Steam Railway and Riverboat Company.

Left: Kingswear Castle & Waverley *meet on the River Medway during a Paddle Steamer Parade event*

Homewaters

Waverley still spends her main season from late June until the end of August at home on the Clyde. Her innovative programme of 1975 has gradually evolved but the essential features continue. Families can still sail from the heart of Glasgow to the traditional resorts of Rothesay and Dunoon. The breathtaking passage through the Kyles of Bute never fails to make a lasting impression on the tourist, while the crossings to Brodick and Campbeltown provide a real "deep sea" experience.

The Clyde can still produce the unexpected. On the last Sunday in September 1992 *Waverley* became the first steamer since March 1940 to call at the tiny fishing village of Carradale. Amazingly, her arrival was captured on film by a photographer who, as a boy, had witnessed the previous call 52 years earlier! The following Easter another innovation devised by Captain Michel brought out the public in their hundreds. Otter Ferry Pier, last used by a passenger steamer in 1914, was found to

be in surprisingly good condition and permission for *Waverley* to call was generously given by the owners. At 1440 on Easter Sunday, Captain Michel gently brought the steamer alongside (left).

Above: Waverley *leaving Brodick, 1993*
Below: Waverley *departing Portencross Pier in 1995, the first time a Paddle Steamer had visited since 1914*

Above: Waverley off Dunoon on Pier Centenary Day 1998
Top right: Waverley passing Finnieston and heading upriver 1995
Middle right: Waverley at Uig, Isle of Skye 1995
Bottom right: Waverley approaching Arrochar

Over 400 passengers streamed ashore, disturbing the tranquility of Loch Fyne with their clicking camera shutters. It was an emotional farewell as *Waverley* left for home, giving the traditional three long blasts on her steam whistle.

To the astonishment of many, two piers which closed in the early 1970s have reappeared in *Waverley's* cruise programme.

In the north of Arran, the new berth at Lochranza has allowed the favourite route via the Kyles of Bute to be revived.

One of the piers visited by *Waverley* on her maiden voyage was Blairmore, at the mouth of Loch Long. As a result of a vigorous local campaign, sufficient funds were raised to restore the structure, allowing regular calls to resume in May 2005.

A Legend reborn

By the mid 1990s, continually escalating maintenance costs and new marine safety requirements were threatening *Waverley's* long term future. Plans were drawn up which would allow the vessel to be rebuilt to an "as new" condition, restoring much of her original character but, at the same time, incorporating modern safety equipment. The work was carried out in two stages over the winters 1999-2000 and 2002-2003.

The Heritage Lottery Fund supported the project and significant funding was also provided by the PSPS, the European Regional Development Fund and various local councils and Enterprise Companies in the west of Scotland.

Tenders were received from five ship repair yards throughout the UK, with George Prior Engineering of Great Yarmouth being awarded the contract. Just before Christmas 1999 *Waverley* arrived at Prior's yard to be "rebuilt". Within a few days many of the ship's fittings had been stripped out. The replacement furniture and upholstery would be a faithful reproduction of the original designs. In early February, 2000, she moved to a drydock across the River Yare. This was the narrowest drydock she had ever been in – she could only get in after her paddleboxes and sponsons had been removed.

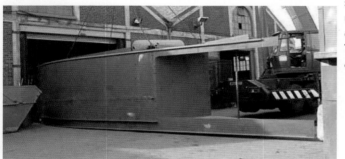

Top right: Waverley's port sponson (now the Gents toilet) under construction at George Prior's (Hull)
Bottom left: After drydocking at Great Yarmouth, the sponson has been fitted
Bottom right: One of the new funnels ready to be fitted in place

Above: An aerial view taken in mid May (14 weeks to sailing) highlights the extent of the rebuild in progress. Three of the four sponsons are in position. Later, a wooden deck will be laid on top and the new after deckhouse fitted. To comply with modern safety regulations a new escape stairway from the Dining Saloon was required.

Top right: Waverley's new funnels have been installed and the painting begins

Bottom right: Painting of Waverley's iconic red, white and black funnels begins

The hull and superstructure were extensively shotblasted, inside and outside. Replacement of corroded steel plates was extensive, as can be seen in this view of the boiler room below, but, perhaps surprisingly, much of the original 1946 plating was found to be fit for further service and retained.

During January 2000, the ship's huge triple expansion engine was dismantled and lifted ashore for renovation. Although the major components were renovated in Great Yarmouth, many smaller items were treated elsewhere. Refurbishment of various pumps, for example, was carried out by Waverley's own engineers at the workshops in Glasgow, while other pieces of equipment were sub-contracted to specialist firms.

By mid-summer the various components were brought together at Great Yarmouth, and re-assembly began.

Top left: One of the new boilers fitted - designed and manufactured by Cochran Boilers of Annan

Top right: New paddle wheels fitted with a heavy weight crane in July 2000

The second phase involved placing her on a barge to allow work on the hull to be undertaken.

This part of the project concentrated on the forward end of the ship. A new deck shelter was fitted and the "Jeanie Deans" Lounge was refurbished. Also, the crew accommodation was extensively redesigned, giving greatly improved facilities.

The 8-ton crankshaft was refurbished ashore. On completion, it was lifted aboard, gleaming in the sunlight and ready for another half century of service.

On 9th June 2003, *Waverley* finally departed from Great Yarmouth for the voyage via Aberdeen back to Glasgow. Over £7 million had been spent repairing, restoring and renewing the world's last seagoing paddle steamer. Undoubtedly her original builders would have approved of the rebirth of the legend they had created.

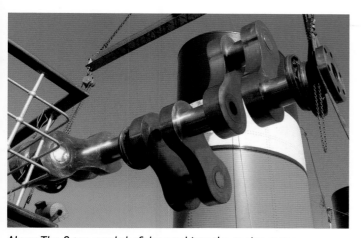

Above: The 8-ton crankshaft lowered into the engine room
Below: The bridge and forward deck shelter start to take shape

Above: The new crew accomodation
Below: Waverley on the barge during the second phase rebuild

Life of the "new" *Waverley*

Life following *Waverley's* heritage rebuild continued in much the same way as previous decades – a series of trials and triumphs.

It had been envisaged at the time of the application to the Heritage Lottery Fund that winter refit costs would be significantly reduced by the rebuild, but this was not the case. The ship's insurance costs increased as she was now more valuable, evolving legislation continued to be an increasing financial burden and with the responsibility of owning a ship which had received so much public investment, came the burden of trying to maintain her in her newly restored condition.

The annual overhauls were no less costly, in fact they became more so.

Sourcing spare parts and finding the skills to repair a paddle steamer's unique features had become nearly impossible and this was never more apparent than in 2008 when *Waverley's* paddle shaft failed following her Western Isles sailings. After much searching, only three companies capable of undertaking the task of repairing the Ship were found.

One in Poland, where three weeks' notice had to be given before the paddle wheel could be transported through the EU; one in Sheffield where work could not start for 3 months; and one in Manchester ready to start within 3 weeks. *Waverley* was out of service for 56 days. The financial impact was considerable with the summer weather being the worst in the UK for 50 years.

This had a catastrophic effect but with the help of the Paddle Steamer Preservation Society, the ship was able to sail for another year.

Fuel costs also impacted on exploring new areas and the "first

Above: The new Gravesend Pontoon at Town Pier

calls" at ports and piers prevalent in previous decades were diminished, though (with money tight everywhere) it should be noted that the reluctance of some councils and other bodies to maintain piers was also a factor.

There were still some first calls of note in almost all of *Waverley's* traditional sailing areas. *Waverley* called at the newly reopened Blairmore Pier. Newport Council provided a berth on the River Usk where *Waverley* was able to call. Inverie, Gairloch and the new pier at Raasay were added into the Steamer's Western Isles programme. *Waverley* used Fairlie while Largs Pier was rebuilt and began to use the new Keppel Pier (the first time in 42 years) on Great Cumbrae when the Town Pier at Millport was closed to major vessels. On the Thames, the long-awaited Gravesend Town Pier opened to welcome *Waverley* passengers. The ship's timetable will always be affected by pier availability and this particular decade recorded the temporary loss (and welcome return) of sailings from Swanage.

Life remained tough financially for *Waverley's* operators. After being saved by her supporters and Lottery winners Chris and Colin Weir, some tough decisions had to be taken. After a financially draining operating season in the notoriously weather-exposed Bristol Channel, the decision was taken to sell *Waverley's* "sister" ship *M.V. Balmoral* for £1 to her new charitable owners M.V. Balmoral Fund Ltd. In turn this would prevent further financial loss to *Waverley*, and therefore protect *Waverley's* future.

Since her rebuild, *Waverley* won many accolades. She was given UKFX Chairman's Award for Tourism, voted Glasgow's Favourite Attraction, awarded 4 stars by Visit Scotland, won the 65th IMechE Engineering Heritage Award and was nominated a "Top 3 nostalgic journey in the world" by the Sunday Times.

Occasion special events and sailings have continued to attract good passenger loadings. 2014 marked the 40th anniversary since the sale of *Waverley* for £1 in 2014, The PSPS (Scottish Branch) arranged a special sailing with *Waverley* visiting the North Ayrshire port of Ardrossan. She left the harbour only a few passengers short of compliment. A new landing stage was built at the end of the Grade II Victorian Pier at Llandudno and after an unfortunate non-call at the Pier due to weather and sea conditions in 2014, *Waverley* boarded passengers on 1st September 2015 for a cruise of the Anglesey Coast. Llandudno sailings have continued to be popular with the public.

In 2015, *Waverley* celebrated her 40th Ruby Anniversary of sailing in Preservation and a reception to celebrate this achievement was held aboard *Waverley* on the 21st May. The celebrations continued in 2017, where she celebrated 70 years since her maiden voyage. This special anniversary year was, however, a little spoiled by an 11-day period off-service due to the failure of an integral part of the system which runs the ship's engines - the air pump. 2018 could only be better for *Waverley*.

A £800,000 repair to the pierhead at Yarmouth in 2018 enabled *Waverley* to return to the Isle of Wight as per recent years. Yarmouth Pier along with Swanage Pier on the south coast look set to welcome *Waverley* for some years to come but unfortunately Bournemouth Pier now looks set to remain closed as a calling point for *Waverley*.

Top: Waverley *going astern from Llandudno Pier*
Middle: Waverley *at Yarmouth Pier*
Bottom: Waverley *at Bournemouth Pier in 2016 - the year of her last visit to Bournemouth*

Withdrawn from service

The planned winter maintenance works during 2018-19 continued as normal with annual surveys booked with legislators and drydock booked for April 2019. During a 10-year boiler survey, structural defects were discovered within Waverley's 20-year-old twin boilers. A repair schedule was implemented with the full intention of the repairs being completed successfully in time for Waverley's operating season: ports and piers were contacted, timetables were released, and even crew were selected for the season ahead.

As the work progressed it became evident that the repairs were becoming more complex, costly and offered no long-term guarantee. It was clear that replacement boilers were required. As a result, the Board of Directors of Waverley Excursions Ltd. and Waverley Steam Navigation Co. Ltd. made the devastating and

difficult decision to withdraw Waverley from service for 2019 – the first full season withdrawal since 1974!

Pre-booked passengers, ticket agents, suppliers and contractors were swiftly contacted to advise that Waverley would not be operating in 2019, and a boiler refit schedule & cost was compiled. In order to replace the boilers, Waverley would undergo "open heart surgery" - her signature red, white and black funnels would need to be removed and areas of the ship's Promenade Deck removed also. Given the scale of the project and the purpose to extend Waverley's operational life, other key boiler-room components would require replacing including the ship's generators and main switchboard in the engine room.

Whilst the magnitude of the refit grew more and more complex,

Left :"Save the Waverley" Boiler Refit Appeal Launch Day by Hugh Dougherty. Bottom: Over 300 Supporters from all over the UK came to the Appeal Launch Day to show their support

equally did the cost of the refit schedule – a total of £2.3 million! For a charity with limited-to-no reserves, a public appeal was launched to "Save the Waverley" on the 15th June 2019. Over 300 supporters boarded *Waverley* at the Glasgow Science Centre to show their support including local & national Press as well as Jackie Baillie MSP & Neil Bibby MSP.

The immediate reaction to the news by the public was very encouraging and donations flooded in from all over the world. *Waverley's* predicament was raised during First Minister questions in the Scottish Parliament and First Minister Nicola Sturgeon MSP stated "The *Waverley* is, of course, a tremendous asset and a great national treasure; we should all want to see it preserved and continue for many years to come."

By mid-July, one month after the Appeal launch, donations received allowed the deposit for the boilers to be made and by August, the new generators were ordered. After receiving tenders from a number of suppliers, the boilers would be built and designed by Cochran Ltd of Annan who built *Waverley's* boilers 20 years prior.

Above: Culture Secretary Fiona Hyslop MSP announcing the Scottish Government's support of £1 million

Top right: Fiona Hyslop MSP with the Board of Directors, Engineers & Staff after the Scottish Government's announcement of support

Bottom right: Paul Semple, General Manager for WEL, Eddie Hawthorne, CEO & Group Managing Director for Arnold Clark, Derek Peters, Financial Director for WEL & Cameron Marshall, Chairman for WEL with the £50,000 contribution from Arnold Clark

During the summer months, the first components were lifted from the boiler-room by crane with a section of the deck cut open to gain access. *Waverley's* stalwart Engineers & Volunteers removed extensive piping in preparation for the refit.

Fundraising efforts to raise funds for the "Save the *Waverley*" Appeal included sponsored 10K runs, cocktail parties, book stalls, home-baking sales, donated souvenir goods, and a sponsored 5 mile cycle ride (8 year old Xander Sclater) just to name a few.

In addition to the donations received by the public & members of the Paddle Steamer Preservation Society, the Society itself provided a grant of £150,000 from their reserves towards the purchase of the boilers and generators. The support didn't stop there.

On the 21st September, only 3 months after the Appeal launch, the Scottish Government announced their support to ensure *Waverley* would operate with £1 million being provided. Culture Secretary Fiona Hyslop MSP, came aboard *Waverley* to announce this news and stated "The *Waverley* has delighted generations of locals and visitors throughout its 70-year history and I am pleased to be able to announce this significant financial commitment to help the historic paddle steamer set sail once again."

At that moment in time, the Appeal had accomplished a total of £1.9 million, and subsequently a provisional booking was made for *Waverley* to attend Dales Marine Shipyard, Greenock in January 2020 for the extensive works to begin. Enthusiasts from all over the UK arranged fundraisers to raise awareness of *Waverley's* cause whilst raising funds for the Appeal. All donors to the Appeal have been recognised on the Donor Wall aboard Waverley today.

Christmas came early for Paddle Steamer *Waverley* as it was announced on the 18th December 2019, after only 6 months of fundraising, that the "Save the Waverley Boiler Refit Appeal" total target of £2.3 million was achieved. Thanks to over 8,500 individuals, the Paddle Steamer Preservation Society, Arnold Clark & the Scottish Government, *Waverley* was saved! The hard work was only about to begin...

Above: 4 year old Ethan Pringle did a 10 mile fundraising trip around the Isle of Cumbrae in his wheelchair and raised over £1,700 to the Appeal

Above: Souvenir Items donated to raise funds. The image was drawn by artist Stephen Millership & products were donated by Doon the Watter - Dunoon

Boiler Refit 2020

On 14th January 2020 *Waverley* was towed from her Glasgow Science Centre berth to Dales Marine Services shipyard at James Watt Dock in Greenock for her boiler refit to begin. After some strenuous project planning and measuring, *Waverley's* iconic twin funnels were removed one by one and gently laid horizontally on the quayside on a cushion of wood & foam. The 6 lifting points on each funnel were load tested to 2 tonnes.

The fiddley deck around the funnels was subsequently removed as well as the various pipes and other fittings positioned under the deck. Within the boiler room there was significant progress with cables being disconnected and the old boiler control consoles being dismantled.

A heavy lift crane arrived on 28th January to remove both boilers. Both boilers weighed in at just over 18 tonnes although the boiler lifting points were load tested to 25 tonnes. Her old boilers were swiftly removed by low-loader and taken to John R Adam scrap yard at King George V dock.

On March 2nd *Waverley* was moved into Garvel dry dock, Greenock. Some steel renewals in the boiler room were carried out as well as her annual hull survey work and hull painting. Three new generators were installed before Waverley was moved back to James Watt Dock ready for her new boilers.

Departing the Glasgow Science Centre under tow

Removal of aft funnel

Left: 28th January 2020 - Removal of one of her 20 year old boilers that had seen better days

Empty boiler room

Above: Fresh lick of paint at Garvel dry dock without her funnels
Below: The forward funnel is lifted over Waverley before being lowered into position. The distance between the funnels had to be precise.

Above: The lowering of her starboard boiler into the correct position
Below: Waverley's new boiler room providing a future for Waverley

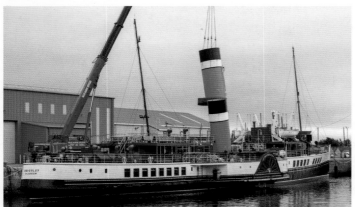

Return to service

Upon completion of the extensive refit, sea trials were carried out to prove the new equipment was satisfactory, crew drills were performed, and passenger certificates were issued. After almost 2 years off-service, *Waverley* set sail on Saturday 22nd August 2020 for her first public sailing carrying a limited number of passengers due to the COVID-19 pandemic. *Waverley* departed the Glasgow Science Centre calling at Blairmore before cruising up Loch Long & Loch Goil. Above she passes under Erskine Bridge dressed to celebrate such an achievement. But as her past has shown us, *Waverley's* story won't end here.

waverleyexcursions.co.uk

9 781916 875210